Eat Your Science
HOMEWORK

Recipes for Inquiring Minds

Ann McCallum

Illustrated by Leeza Hernandez

Charlesbridge

To Rich—and to the best family ever.—A. M.

For my great and oh-so-sciency Dad!—L. H.

Table of Contents

Yum!

Discovering Delicious

There you are, minding your own business in science class. You look at the clock: only a couple minutes until the bell rings. Phew! You've made it through class without the teacher assigning any homework. But wait—she's writing something on the chalkboard. Oh no! Homework. Science homework! Your heart sinks—until you remember a surefire way to turn toil into tasty and drudgery into delicious. Today after school you can turn the tables (er, not the periodic table) by EATING your science homework!

This is a book about edible science projects. Each section includes a method—a step-by-step recipe—to make a yummy science treat. The recipes are easy to medium in ability level, and they tie into many of the branches of science. Experiment with fun facts and "science samplers," and you'll soon discover that doing science homework is a piece of cake!

Note: Words in **bold** can be found in the glossary on page 44.

A Method to the Science

Scientists ask questions about the world around them. They use a process called the **scientific method** to help them discover answers. For example:

Ask a *question*. [Will the recipes in this book be delicious?]

⬇

Make a *hypothesis*, or guess. [Yes, I do think the recipes will be mighty tasty.]

⬇

Experiment to test the hypothesis. [Make the recipes for yourself.]

⬇

Observe and analyze what happens. [Gee, nobody can resist this food. It's already all gone!]

⬇

State your *conclusion*. [Yep, following these recipes means scrumptious food for all.]

Safety in the Lab . . . er, Kitchen

Time to put on your lab coat and cook up some tasty experiments! But remember that it's "safety first." Always ask an adult to assist you, and stick to these basic rules to keep yourself and others safe.

- Read all the directions and gather all the right equipment *before* you begin a recipe.
- Ask for assistance with anything sharp or hot, and leave the oven or stove to adults.
- Make sure you have a large enough work space.
- Keep things clean (including your hands!).

Tricks of the Trade:

- Have an adult preheat the oven so it's just the right temperature when you're ready to use it.
- Start with ingredients that are at room temperature, like butter or margarine.

- Measure ingredients carefully. Mix dry ingredients (flour, sugar, etc.) first and then wet ingredients (butter, milk, etc.), so the dry ingredients won't stick to the wet surfaces of the measuring tools.
- Gradually add dry ingredients to wet ones a little at a time, and mix thoroughly between each addition.

Now, ready, set . . . Let's go eat some science homework!

Atomic Popcorn Balls

Miniature, minuscule, microscopic . . . What's the smallest thing you can see in your house? A thumbtack? A grain of salt? A speck of dust under your bed? Sure, these things may seem small to us, but if you *really* want to talk tiny, think about an **atom**. All **matter** is made of atoms, the building blocks of Earth. Inside every atom are **subatomic** particles. The **nucleus** in the center of an atom contains **protons** and **neutrons**. Even smaller **electrons** circle around this center. But how small is small? Take this page between your thumb and forefinger. It would take about one *million* atoms stacked on top of each other to equal the thickness of just this one page!

Most matter is made up of a combination of different kinds of atoms linked together. **Elements** are substances composed of only one type of atom. These pure substances are listed on a chart called the **Periodic Table of Elements**. On this table, elements have a special symbol and atomic number, and are arranged according to their properties. When elements bond together they form **molecules**—a unit of at least two atoms. Hydrogen (H), the first element, is the most common element on Earth. Put two hydrogen atoms together with one oxygen atom and you get one molecule of H_2O. Can you guess what this is? (Hint: You can drink it or wash the dog with it.) Hungry for more? Turn the page for a truly *molecular* experience.

Atomic Popcorn Balls

BEFORE YOU BEGIN

Prep time: 15 minutes
Cooking time: 5 minutes
Total time: 20 minutes

Oven temperature: n/a
Yield: varies
Difficulty: medium

INGREDIENTS

- 2 tablespoons butter, plus a little extra butter or cooking spray
- 2 cups miniature marshmallows
- ½ cup light corn syrup
- A few drops food coloring in two different colors
- 6 heaping cups popped popcorn [IMPORTANT: Remove all unpopped kernels!]
- Optional: ½ cup dried fruit, such as raisins, cherries, etc.

EQUIPMENT

Cookie sheet or tray
Medium-sized saucepan
Wooden spoon or spatula
Two large mixing bowls
Toothpicks

METHOD

1 Grease a cookie sheet or tray with butter or cooking spray.

2 Have an adult help you melt the butter in a medium-sized saucepan on the stove.

3 Add the marshmallows and light corn syrup to the butter. Stir constantly until the marshmallows melt.

4 Divide the marshmallow mixture into two large bowls. Add a few drops of food coloring to each bowl and mix thoroughly.

5 Carefully stir in the popped popcorn—with no unpopped kernels!—into each bowl, three heaping cups in each. If desired, add in the dried fruit now, too. Make sure the popcorn is completely coated with the marshmallow mixture. Allow it to cool slightly. *(Take a deep whiff. What can you say about smell and states of matter?)*

6 Spray your clean hands with cooking spray. When the popcorn mixture is cool enough to handle, grab a handful from one of the bowls and form it into a ball. Place the popcorn ball on the greased tray. Repeat until all the popcorn and marshmallow mixture is used up.

7 Make "molecules" by using toothpicks to secure the "atoms" together. For example, to make a water molecule, join two similarly colored popcorn balls to one ball of the other color. Presto—you've made the world's first *solid* water molecule!

Science Sampler

Now that you have bonded popcorn elements together, can you find these common elements around your house?

11	13	20	28	29	47
Na	Al	Ca	Ni	Cu	Ag
Sodium	Aluminum	Calcium	Nickel	Copper	Silver

Not to State the Obvious, But . . .

All matter occurs naturally in one of three common conditions, or **states**: gas, solid, or liquid. Under the right conditions, matter can change from one state to another. A kernel of popcorn is actually the seed of a corn plant, kept alive with a tiny amount of moisture inside the kernel. With high, sudden heat, this liquid turns into steam—a gas. The gas expands, and VOILÀ!—the pressure causes the kernel to burst open. Lucky us!

Periodic Table of the Elements

H																	He
Li	Be											B	C	N	O	F	Ne
Na	Mg											Al	Si	P	S	Cl	Ar
K	Ca	Sc	Ti	V	Cr	Mn	Fe	Co	Ni	Cu	Zn	Ga	Ge	As	Se	Br	Kr
Rb	Sr	Y	Zr	Nb	Mo	Tc	Ru	Rh	Pd	Ag	Cd	In	Sn	Sb	Te	I	Xe
Cs	Ba	La	Hf	Ta	W	Re	Os	Ir	Pt	Au	Hg	Tl	Pb	Bi	Po	At	Rn
Fr	Ra	Ac	Rf	Db	Sg	Bh	Hs	Mt	Ds	Rg	Cn	Uut	Fl	Uup	Lv	Uus	Uuo

Ce	Pr	Nd	Pm	Sm	Eu	Gd	Tb	Dy	Ho	Er	Tm		
Th	U	Np							Es	Fm	Md		

Density Dressing and Veggie Sticks

There's a certain chemistry between oil and vinegar. Or rather, there isn't. Oil and vinegar have such different chemical structures that there will never be a "marriage" between the two. Toss together some oil and vinegar for your salad dressing, and you'll soon see that unless you shake them together constantly, these two liquids will separate and form layers. These two substances are said to be **immiscible**. No matter how long you let the liquids sit, they will not mix together. Liquids that *will* eventually combine together are called **miscible**.

It's true—oil and vinegar *don't* mix. It's all because of their properties of matter—or the characteristics that describe what they are made of. In this case the chemistry and **density** of each liquid is different. The molecules in vinegar aren't attracted to the molecules in oil. And since oil is denser than vinegar, the oil will sink to the bottom when the two liquids are put together. To understand density, look at a sugar cube and a miniature marshmallow. About the same size, right? But the sugar weighs more than the marshmallow because it's much denser. Density refers to how tightly packed something is. Think of a milkshake versus a glass of water, or a bowl of thick stew versus a bowl of clear broth. The denser the food, the more it's going to fill you up.

Feeling a little empty? Wait until you bulk up on some tasty Density Dressing and Veggie Sticks!

Density Dressing and Veggie Sticks • • • • •

Before You Begin

Prep time: 15 minutes
Cooking time: 0 minutes
Total time: 15 minutes

Oven temperature: n/a
Yield: 3–4 servings
(1–2 veggie sticks per person)
Difficulty: easy

Ingredients

- 1 tablespoon honey
- 1 tablespoon barbeque sauce
- 3 tablespoons vinegar and 2 drops food coloring
- 3 tablespoons vegetable oil
- Salt and pepper to taste
- Raw vegetables for the veggie sticks, such as grape tomatoes, olives, pepper chunks, etc.

Equipment

Tall, narrow glass
Small mixing bowl
Skewers or
kebab sticks

Method

1. Add the honey to a tall, narrow glass. Carefully pour in the barbeque sauce.

2. In a small mixing bowl, mix the vinegar and food coloring. Add this to the dressing mixture. *(Are the vinegar and food coloring miscible or immiscible?)*

14

3 Slowly pour in the vegetable oil. Season the mixture with salt and pepper. Let the dressing sit while you thread the veggies on the skewers, alternating as you go. *(What's happening with the dressing now?)*

4 When you arc ready to serve the dressing, cover the top of the glass, and shake or stir vigorously. Dip the veggie sticks to coat them with the dressing.

Yum! Work quickly, though, because the ingredients in the dressing will want to separate again.

Professor Zh

16

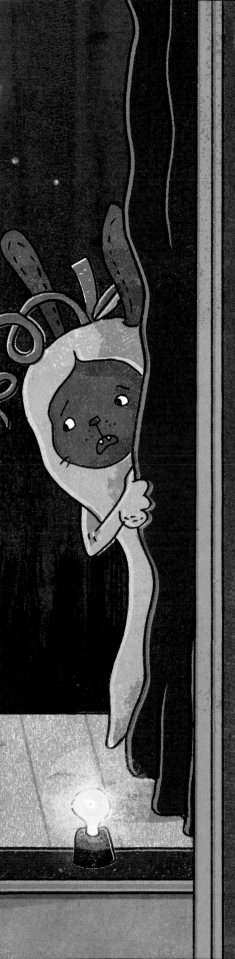

Science Sampler

Once you've devoured your Density Dressing,
how about trying this density dilemma?

Ask an adult for assistance and combine
a small amount of each of the following
liquid pairs in narrow glasses:

1. Vegetable oil
   and milk

2. Vegetable oil and diet soda

3. Vegetable oil and rubbing alcohol

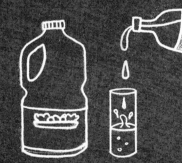

Wait, and you'll see they are immiscible—the liquids
separate. What can you say about the density of these
liquid pairs?

(If you said that the denser liquid sinks to the bottom,
you are one hundred percent correct. Hoorah!)

Invisible Ink Snack Pockets

In 1869 Henry Solomon Wellcome placed an advertisement for a mysterious invisible ink in his local newspaper. Was it magic? What was his secret formula? Actually Henry's "invisible ink" was nothing more than lemon juice—undetectable when used to write on paper, but easily seen once the paper was brought near a heat source. Alas, Henry did not make a million bucks selling his invisible ink—but he did become famous!

Since Henry's time people have experimented with different kinds of invisible ink—and with different methods for making it visible. Many colorless liquids will appear with the presence of heat. A mixture of sugar and water works well. The sugar will caramelize with heat in a chemical process called **oxidation**, which breaks down the sugar compound and re-forms the molecules in a darker color.

Acidic liquids go through oxidation, too. All liquids are acids, bases, or neutral. Scientists use the **pH scale** to measure how acidic or basic a liquid is. Whether a liquid is an acid or base depends on the type of ions in it. An **ion** is an atom or molecule that does not have an equal number of electrons and protons. If the liquid has more hydrogen ions, then it is an acid—like lemon juice. If it has more hydroxide ions, then it is a base—like bleach. Although you can use other chemicals or ultraviolet light to create and reveal invisible ink, heat-activated invisible ink tends to be acidic. Whichever method you choose, invisible ink is a great way to keep things private!

Secret
Code:
694

TOP

Invisible Ink Snack Pockets • • • • • • • •

BEFORE YOU BEGIN

Prep time: 10 minutes
Cooking time: 5–7 minutes and
1–1½ minutes
Total time: 18½ minutes

Oven temperature: 425° and low broil
Yield: 3 servings
Difficulty: medium

INGREDIENTS

- 1 package refrigerated thin-crust pizza dough
- Shredded cheese—mozzarella or cheddar work well
- Optional add-ins such as ham, mushrooms, green pepper, crumbled bacon, etc.
- ½ teaspoon baking soda
- 1 tablespoon sugar
- Enough water to make a paste (about 2 teaspoons)

EQUIPMENT

Cutting board
Knife
Cookie sheet or tray
Cotton swab or new paintbrush

METHOD

1 Ask an adult to preheat the oven to 425° Fahrenheit.

2 Unroll the dough onto a clean cutting board. Cut rectangular sections about 3 inches by 5 inches.

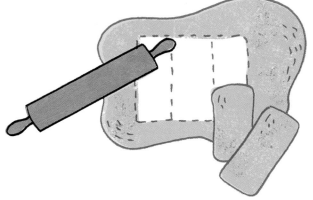

3 Spread a generous sprinkling of cheese onto each rectangle. Place the add-ins of your choice on the dough.

4 Carefully fold over the dough to make a square pocket. Place each pocket on a cookie tray, two inches apart.

5 Prepare the "invisible ink." Make a runny paste with the baking soda, sugar, and water. Dip a cotton swab or new paintbrush into the ink and print something on the top of each roll-over snack.

6 Ask an adult to place the roll-over snacks on the top shelf of the oven for about 5–7 minutes. Then, for 1 to 1 ½ additional minutes, turn the oven on LOW broil. (Watch carefully so they don't burn!) Remove the snacks as soon as the invisible writing appears.

Does your oven have a glass door so you can watch the roll-ups bake? How long did it take for the ink to appear?

Invisible Ink Snack Pockets

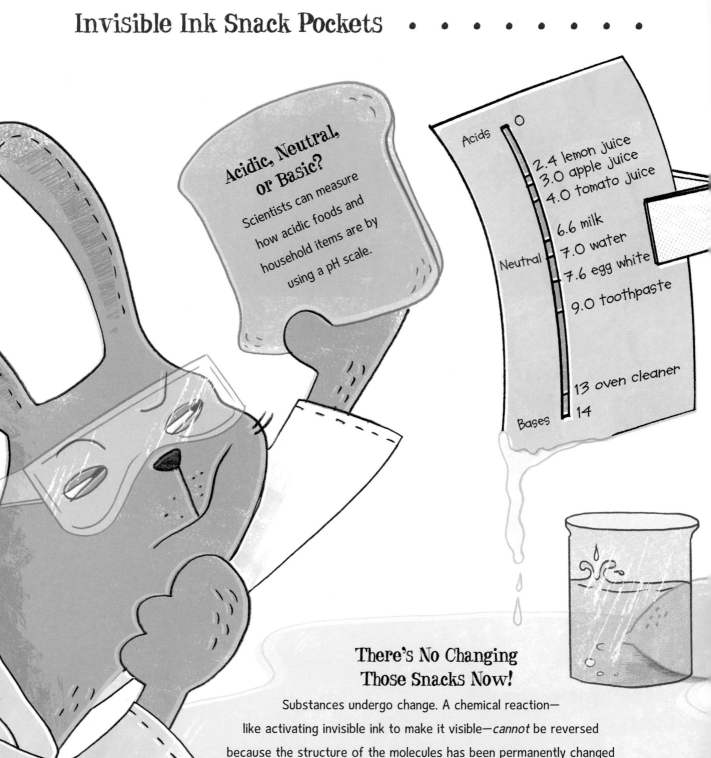

Acidic, Neutral, or Basic?

Scientists can measure how acidic foods and household items are by using a pH scale.

Acids

0

2.4 lemon juice
3.0 apple juice
4.0 tomato juice

6.6 milk
7.0 water
7.6 egg white

Neutral

9.0 toothpaste

13 oven cleaner

Bases

14

There's No Changing Those Snacks Now!

Substances undergo change. A chemical reaction—
like activating invisible ink to make it visible—*cannot* be reversed
because the structure of the molecules has been permanently changed
(example: pizza dough to baked dough). In a physical reaction,
a substance *can* be changed back to its original state (example:
solid cheese to melted cheese and back to solid cheese).

Science Sampler

Question: What colorless, edible liquids will become visible when heat is added?

Make a hypothesis.

Experiment: Open the fridge and check out some invisible-ink possibilities. (Hint: Try milk, apple juice, or vinegar). Dip a cotton swab into your chosen "ink" and write a message on a blank sheet of paper. When the ink is dry, hold the paper near a heat source, such as a lighted bulb (ask an adult for help).

 or or

Observe and analyze.

Conclude: What happened? Which liquid will you use to write your next secret message?

23

Loop, Whorl, and Arch Cookies

Who stole the cookies from the cookie jar? The next time someone accuses *you* of cookie-stealing, you may want to turn to **forensic** science. You can prove your case by using fingerprint evidence.

Every person has a unique pattern of ridges on his or her fingers. Unlike other parts of your body, your fingerprints remain the same throughout your life. The pattern your fingerprints make can be classified into a few basic types: loops, whorls, or arches.

If you look carefully at the surface of the skin on your fingertips, you'll see what's called **friction ridge skin**. When investigators compare fingerprints, they look for where these ridges end or branch into a different direction. These marked areas are called **minutiae**. The oils on your fingertips leave distinct marks on nearly everything you touch. Check it out: run your fingers through your hair to attract extra oil, and press them against the glass in a mirror or window. Look carefully. Did you leave fingerprints? (If anyone comments on the dirty fingerprints you've left behind, inform them that you are conducting a scientific investigation—and then politely rub them off, of course!)

Coming up: Loop, Whorl, and Arch Cookies— a sweet way to make your mark.

Loop, Whorl, and Arch Cookies • • • • • • • •

BEFORE YOU BEGIN

Prep time: 15 minutes
Cooking time: 8–12 minutes
Total time: 27 minutes

Oven temperature: 375°
Yield: 12 large cookies
Difficulty: medium

INGREDIENTS

- ½ cup butter, at room temperature
- ¾ cup sugar
- 1 egg
- 2 tablespoons frozen orange juice concentrate (once it's thawed enough)
- ¼ teaspoon salt
- 2 cups flour
- M&M candies

EQUIPMENT

Large mixing bowl
Electric mixer or spatula
Rolling pin
Cutting board
Small glass or round cookie cutter
Cookie sheet

METHOD

1 Ask an adult to preheat the oven to 375° Fahrenheit.

2 In a large bowl, first beat together the butter and sugar. Then mix in the egg and orange juice concentrate.

3 Add the salt and flour. Mix thoroughly.

4 Gather the dough together with your (clean) hands and knead for several seconds. Using a rolling pin, roll the dough so that it is about ¼ inch thick. (Hint: Sprinkle flour on the cutting board and on the rolling pin ahead of time. This prevents the dough from sticking.)

5 Use an inverted glass or round cookie cutter to cut circles from the dough.

6 Place each circle on a lightly greased cookie sheet. Put a few M&M candies in the center of each cutout cookie. (Use different amounts and colors because, just like people, no two cookies are exactly the same.) Set another dough circle directly on top.

7 With your (clean) thumb, make fingerprints on the edges of the dough: Press the edges of the top and bottom dough circles so the pieces are sealed together. Put another M&M candy on top of the cookie sandwich for decoration.

8 With adult assistance, place the cookie sheet in the oven. Bake 8 to 12 minutes. Remove and allow the cookies to cool on the cookie sheet.

Loop, Whorl, and Arch Cookies

The Daily Whorl

EXCLUSIVE

Cookie Thief, Guilty by Fingerprint

Loop

Whorl

Arch

Fingerprint Facts

Using fingerprint evidence to arrest and convict crime suspects became popular in the 1800s. In 1911, in a landmark case in the United States, Thomas Jennings was found guilty of murder based on fingerprint evidence. Today in the United States, crime investigators use the Integrated Automated Fingerprint Identification System to help solve crimes. There are more than forty million fingerprints in this system, and hundreds more are added every day.

Science Sampler

Question: Are the type of fingerprints you have an inherited trait?

⬇

Make a hypothesis.

⬇

Experiment: Get a pencil, a piece of sandpaper, and some clear tape. Press your thumb onto a smooth plate or glass. Rub your pencil along the sandpaper to get a little graphite dust. Gently sprinkle the dust onto the fingerprint, blowing off the excess. Take a section of tape and lift off the print. Tape the print onto a piece of paper. Do the same for the rest of your family members. (Don't forget to label who's who!)

⬇

Observe each print closely (use a magnifying glass if you have one). Analyze whether each is a loop, whorl, or arch.

⬇

Conclude: What did you find out?

More on this: Indeed, the type of fingerprints you have may be inherited, though every person has a unique, specific pattern of prints. What other traits are inherited? Look at photos of yourself and your relatives. Even better, try to find photos of your relatives when they were your age. Are there any similarities?

tape

sandpaper

pencil

Sedimentary Pizza Lasagna

All rocks are NOT created equal. There are three basic categories of rocks: **metamorphic, igneous**, and **sedimentary**. Metamorphic rocks morph, or change form, after being exposed to heat and pressure. Igneous rocks form when liquid rock from beneath the earth's surface cools and hardens. Sedimentary rocks develop when layers of sediment (small pieces of rock and minerals) press down on each other and cement together. One thing IS the same, though: all rocks are made up of two or more **minerals**. Minerals are nonliving, naturally occurring solids.

Is all this rock talk making you hungry?

31

Sedimentary Pizza Lasagna • • • • • • • •

BEFORE YOU BEGIN

Prep time: 20 minutes
Cooking time: 45 minutes
Total time: 1 hour 5 minutes

Oven temperature: 375°
Yield: 4–6 servings
Difficulty: medium

EQUIPMENT

Frying pan
Spoon or spatula
Rectangular pan (8 x 10 inches or larger)
Heavy-duty aluminum foil
Small bowl

INGREDIENTS

- ½ pound (8 ounces) ground turkey or beef
- 2 cups pizza sauce
- 1 egg
- 1 cup ricotta cheese
- Oven-ready lasagna noodles
- Sliced pepperoni
- 1–2 cups shredded mozzarella cheese

METHOD

❶ With an adult's help, cook the ground meat in a frying pan until it is brown. Drain off any fat. Add the pizza sauce and mix well.

❷ Ask an adult to preheat the oven to 375°. Spread about ½ cup of the meat sauce on the bottom of the rectangular pan. Top with oven-ready lasagna noodles, overlapping slightly to cover the whole pan. Top with more sauce—about ½ cup.

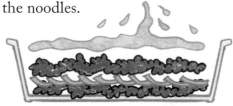

❸ Crack and beat the egg in a separate bowl, then mix thoroughly with ricotta cheese. Spread half this mixture over the noodles.

❹ Arrange a layer of pepperoni next, followed by a sprinkling of cheese. Top with a layer of lasagna noodles.

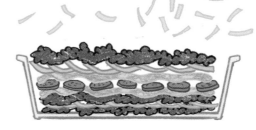

❺ Repeat the layers. Cover the final layer of lasagna noodles with the remaining meat sauce and a generous amount of mozzarella cheese.

❻ Cover the pan with heavy-duty foil. Bake for 45 minutes. Uncover and bake for another 10 minutes. *Can you still identify the individual ingredients?*

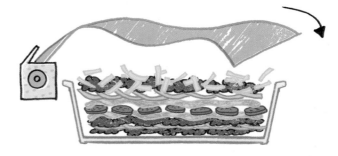

Sedimentary Pizza Lasagna ● ● ● ● ● ● ●

Mohs Scale of Hardness

On a scale of one to ten, how hard is your science homework? Not that kind of hard—we're talking about how firm or rigid something is. Different minerals can be classified according to how hard they are. In 1812 a man named Friedrich Mohs created a rating chart to classify the hardness of minerals. Each higher-numbered mineral on the Mohs Scale of Hardness can scratch the minerals with lower numbers. Can you guess what the hardest mineral is?

Hardness	Mineral	Uses
1	Talc	Talcum powder is used on babies to prevent diaper rash
2	Gypsum	Classroom chalk
3	Calcite	A component of limestone, found in many seashells
4	Fluorite	Contains fluorine, which helps prevent cavities in teeth
5	Apatite	Used when making fertilizer
6	Orthoclase	Used as a gemstone
7	Quartz	Used in making glass
8	Topaz	Used as a gemstone
9	Corundum	Used to make abrasives such as sandpaper or grinding wheels. Rubies and sapphires are corundums.
10	Diamond	Used in wedding rings and cutting tools

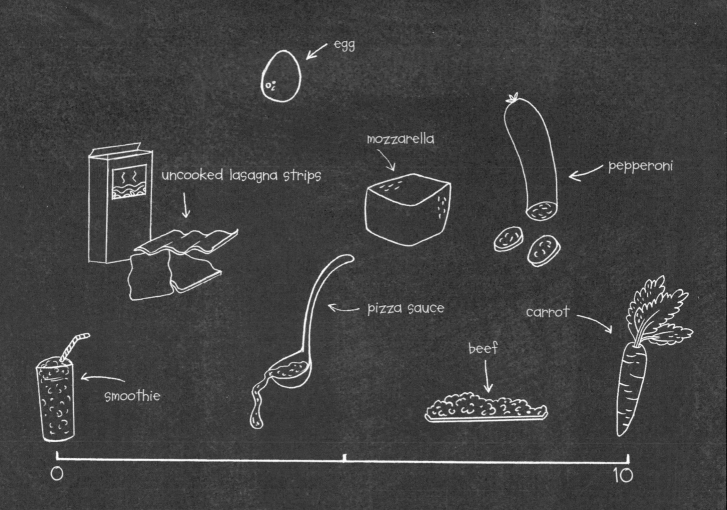

egg

mozzarella

pepperoni

uncooked lasagna strips

pizza sauce

carrot

beef

smoothie

0   10

Science Sampler

When your Sedimentary Pizza Lasagna baked, the ingredients melded together to create a sediment. But before the sediment formed, each ingredient had its own level of hardness. Not only do the ingredients taste different, of course, but some are hard or crisp, and others are soft or silky. You can create a scale like the Mohs Scale to rate items from the recipe and from your fridge. For example, if a carrot is a 10 and a smoothie is a 1, what number would you assign to the ingredients in Sedimentary Pizza Lasagna? Uncooked lasagna noodles? Pizza sauce? A chunk of mozzarella cheese? Chart your results like Friedrich Mohs.

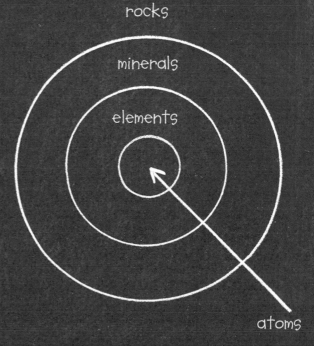

rocks

minerals

elements

atoms

Black Hole Swallow-Ups

Zip, nil, zilch—nothing escapes a **black hole**. To understand black holes, take a piece of stretchy cloth (a sports shirt or bathing suit will work). Have someone else hold the cloth out flat while you place something heavy in the middle. What happened? Did the heavy object make a dent in the fabric? Try something heavier, but still about the same size. Is the dent deeper?

A black hole is like an indentation in space, as if a very heavy force were pressing down on the cloth of space. The **gravity** at the surface of a black hole is like a superstrong vacuum. Anything that gets too close to the black hole is swallowed up and lost forever. Not even light can escape this massive force.

Black holes come in two sizes: very large or very small. Large black holes are formed when a gigantic star (much larger than our sun) explodes and then collapses on itself. This spectacular explosion is called a **supernova**. A supernova can produce as much energy as our own sun will generate over its *entire* lifetime. (But don't worry about the sun dying anytime soon—it still has, oh, five billion years or so left to live.) There's still plenty of time to enjoy some Black Hole Swallow-Ups!

Black Hole Swallow-Ups • • • • • • • • • •

Before You Begin

Prep time: 15 minutes
Cooking time: 12–15 minutes
Total time: 30 minutes

Oven temperature: 375°
Yield: 12 Swallow-Ups
Difficulty: medium

Ingredients

- 1 egg
- 2 tablespoons vegetable oil
- 1 cup pancake mix
- ¼ cup powdered milk
- 1 cup club soda
- ½ cup chopped sausage
- Optional: cooked and crumbled bacon
- Pancake syrup

Equipment

Muffin tin
Paper muffin cups or cooking spray
Medium mixing bowl
Large mixing bowl
Electric mixer or spatula

Method

1. Ask an adult to preheat the oven to 375° Fahrenheit. Prepare a 12-muffin tin by spraying with cooking spray or lining with paper muffin cups.

2. In a medium bowl, beat together egg and vegetable oil.

3. Measure the pancake mix and powdered milk into a large bowl. Add the egg mixture all at once, and stir until combined. Add the club soda, stirring lightly.

4. Fill each muffin tin so that it is ¾ full.

5. Place a spoonful of sausage bits (and crumbled bacon, if desired) on top of each muffin. Let the muffins sit for about 5 minutes.

6. Bake for 12–15 minutes. See how gravity "swallows up" the sausage. The force of gravity pulls the sausage pieces toward the bottom of the muffin tins. Serve warm with syrup.

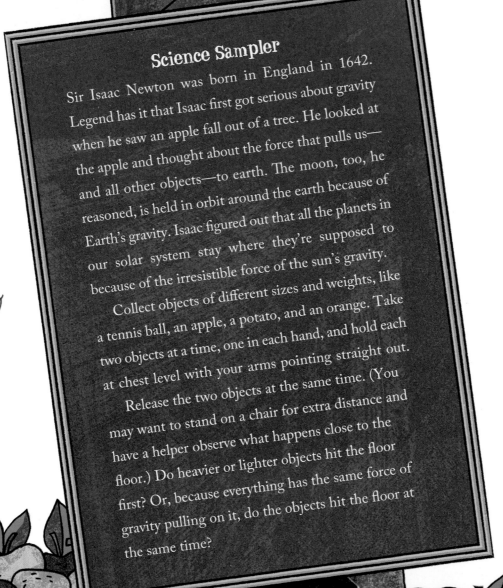

Science Sampler

Sir Isaac Newton was born in England in 1642. Legend has it that Isaac first got serious about gravity when he saw an apple fall out of a tree. He looked at the apple and thought about the force that pulls us—and all other objects—to earth. The moon, too, he reasoned, is held in orbit around the earth because of Earth's gravity. Isaac figured out that all the planets in our solar system stay where they're supposed to because of the irresistible force of the sun's gravity.

Collect objects of different sizes and weights, like a tennis ball, an apple, a potato, and an orange. Take two objects at a time, one in each hand, and hold each at chest level with your arms pointing straight out. Release the two objects at the same time. (You may want to stand on a chair for extra distance and have a helper observe what happens close to the floor.) Do heavier or lighter objects hit the floor first? Or, because everything has the same force of gravity pulling on it, do the objects hit the floor at the same time?

Things with smaller mass are attracted by gravity to things of greater mass. Mass is a measure that always stays the same, but weight depends on where you are, because it relies on gravitational pull. On earth your dog might weigh 45 pounds, but on the moon, where gravity doesn't pull as hard, your canine would weigh a mere 7.4 pounds. That's one petite pooch!

41

Science Review

Was your hypothesis correct? Was all that science food hands-down delicious? Before we leave, here's a quick overview of what we discovered.

The Scientific Method

The scientific method is a step-by-step system for learning something new.

1. Ask a question. 2. Make a hypothesis, or guess. 3. Experiment. 4. Observe and analyze what happens. 5. Form a conclusion: what did you find out?

Atoms and Molecules

An atom is the smallest unit of matter. It is made up of subatomic particles: a nucleus of protons and neutrons, surrounded by electrons.

Elements are pure substances made up of only one kind of atom.

All matter is found in one of three basic states: solid, liquid, or gas. Temperature or pressure can make matter change from one state to another.

Properties of Matter

Substances that will blend together and stay blended are miscible. Substances that won't are immiscible.

Density refers to how tightly packed something is.

Inherited Traits

Forensic science is used to solve crimes and other problems when what happened is not immediately clear.

Friction ridge skin is the raised pattern of lines on the surface of your fingertips. This pattern can be one of three basic types: loops, whorls, or arches.

Traits like hair or skin color, physical features like the shape of your nose, and even some personality traits can be inherited.

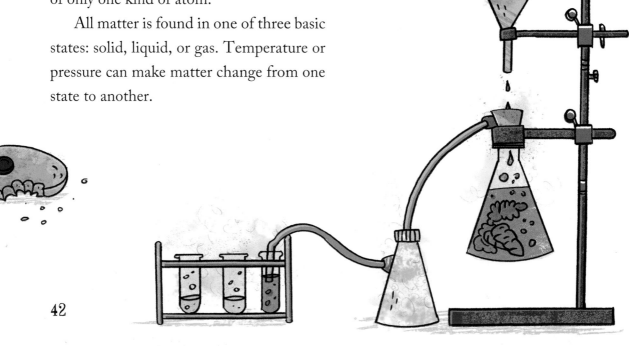

Rocks and Minerals

Metamorphic rock results from heat and pressure. Igneous rock is cooled and hardened from liquid rock. Sedimentary rock forms from layers of smaller rock and sand.

Minerals occur naturally. Their structure is an organized pattern of one or more elements.

Our Solar System

A black hole is a feature in space with a huge gravitational pull.

Mass is the measure of matter in an object, and is the same no matter where you are. Weight can vary, because it depends on gravity.

Gravity is a force that makes the objects on the earth remain on the earth. Gravity pulls everything downward, toward the center of the earth.

43

Glossary

Atom: the smallest particle of an element

Black hole: a mass in space with gravity so strong that even light cannot escape its pull

Compound: a substance consisting of two or more different elements

Density: the concentrated amount of something within a specific area

Electron: the subatomic particle that circles around the nucleus

Element: any pure substance that contains only one type of atom

Friction ridge skin: the pattern of small, raised lines on the skin

Forensic: using science or technology to investigate a crime or problem

Gravity: the force or attraction of a smaller object to a larger object

Hypothesis: an educated guess

Igneous: rock that was created through extreme heat

Immiscible: unable to mix with another substance

Mass: the constant amount of matter an object has, regardless of where it is

Matter: any substance, living or nonliving, that takes up space and has mass

Metamorphic: rock that has been changed through heat or pressure

Mineral: a natural solid made up of elements

Minutiae: the main characteristics of a fingerprint

Miscible: able to combine with another substance

Mohs Scale of Hardness: a chart comparing the hardness of different minerals

Molecule: a unit of two or more atoms, held together with a strong chemical bond

Neutron: a particle inside an atom that has no electric charge

Nucleus: the center of an atom, containing protons and neutrons

Oxidation: a chemical change when a substance reacts to oxygen by losing electrons, such as when silver tarnishes or metal rusts

Periodic Table of Elements: a chart of all the elements

Proton: a particle inside an atom that has a positive electric charge

Scientific method: a step-by-step process for investigating the world around us

Sedimentary: rock formed from smaller particles that have been pressed down in layers and cemented together

State: phases of matter such as solid, liquid, or gas

Subatomic: smaller than an atom

Supernova: an exploding star that produces a huge amount of energy and light

Weight: a measure of how heavy something is, depending on the force of gravity pulling it down

Mmm . . . this Sedimentary Pizza Lasagna rocks!

Index

Published by Charlesbridge
85 Main Street
Watertown, MA 02472
(617) 926-0329
www.charlesbridge.com

Library of Congress Cataloging-in-Publication Data
McCallum, Ann, 1965.
    Eat your science homework: recipes for inquiring minds/Ann McCallum; illustrated by Leeza Hernandez.
      pages cm
    Includes index.
    ISBN 978-1-57091-298-6 (reinforced for library use)
    ISBN 978-1-57091-299-3 (softcover)
    ISBN 978-1-60734-744-6 (ebook)
    ISBN 978-1-60734-626-5 (ebook pdf)
1. Science—Experiments—Juvenile literature. 2. Food—Experiments—Juvenile literature.
3. Food—Composition—Juvenile literature. 4. Cooking—Experiments—Juvenile literature.
I. Hernandez, Leeza, illustrator. II. Title.
Q182.3.M385 2014
507.8—dc23   2013022070

Printed in Singapore
(hc) 10 9 8 7 6 5 4 3 2 1
(sc) 10 9 8 7 6 5 4 3 2 1

Illustrations were created using a mixed media technique
    combining printmaking, pencil, and digital collage.
Display type and text type set in Blue Century,
    Adobe Caslon Pro, Humper, and Soupbone
Color separations by KHL Chroma Graphics, Singapore
Printed and bound February 2014 by Imago in Singapore
Production supervision by Brian G. Walker
Designed by Martha MacLeod Sikkema